T-SHIRT

written by
H. I. Peeples

illustrated by
Michael Moran

A CALICO BOOK
Published by Contemporary Books, Inc.
CHICAGO · NEW YORK

Library of Congress Cataloging-in-Publication Data
Peeples, H. I.
T-shirt / written by H. I. Peeples ; illustrated by Michael Moran.
p.   cm. — (Where does this come from?)
"A Calico book."
Summary: Explains how T-shirts are made, from the harvesting of
the cotton to the customizing of the final product.
ISBN 0-8092-4407-1 : $6.95
1. T-shirts—Juvenile literature.   [1. T-shirts.]
I. Moran, Michael, 1957–   ill.   II. Title.
III. Series: Peeples, H. I.   Where does this come from?
TT675.P44   1989

687′.2—dc19   88-39458
CIP
AC

The Kipling Press would like to thank Fruit of the Loom
for its invaluable assistance in completing this book.

Published by Contemporary Books, Inc.
180 North Michigan Avenue, Chicago, Illinois 60601
Manufactured in the United States of America
Library of Congress Catalog Card Number: 88-39458
International Standard Book Number: 0-8092-4407-1

Published simultaneously in Canada by Beaverbooks, Ltd.
195 Allstate Parkway, Valleywood Business Park
Markham, Ontario L3R 4T8 Canada

I hate zips and buttons, and collars and cuffs. My favorite shirt is a T-shirt, and I bet it's yours, too! But have you ever wondered where T-shirts come from? Listen carefully, because it's a fascinating story. It's all about a small, fluffy white plant called *cotton*, which was first grown many, many years ago by the ancient Egyptians.

The story of the T-shirt is really the story of cotton, because that's what most T-shirts are made of. T-shirts are also made of cotton blended with human-made fibers like polyester, but no one has been able to invent a fiber as soft and as comfortable as cotton.

Cotton grows from small cotton plants with bright pink flowers. It is a gift from nature. Farmers grow the plants and then harvest the cotton. Not long ago, people had to pick cotton by hand. Today we have big machines to do that for us.

The cotton on plants grows in little clumps called *bolls*. The cotton surrounds the plant's seeds and protects them, just as the shell of a walnut protects what's inside. But before the cotton can be used to make clothes, it has to be separated from the seeds. This is done by a machine called a *cotton gin*. The cotton gin was invented by Eli Whitney in 1793, and some people say this was what began the age of machines.

The seedless cotton is then packed into huge bundles called *bales* and delivered to the textile mill. There a *carding machine* combs the fibers with big metal teeth—a bit like combing your hair! The cotton comes out as long, white ropes called *slivers*.

7

Before cotton can be used to make clothes, all the little fibers have to be stretched tight and wound together. This is called *spinning*. Years ago, large spinning wheels were used for this. Today, a machine combines several slivers into a larger rope and sends the rope to a spinning machine. This machine twists and spins the slivers into thinner strands called *yarn*. The yarn is then wound onto cones called *spools*.

Just like an architect who designs a house, or a chef who thinks up a new recipe, a fashion designer is hard at work designing the style and shape of the T-shirt. The designers make patterns for the shirts that the machines will cut out later.

The cloth for the T-shirts is made from many strands of yarn that are knitted together in a loop pattern. The cloth for T-shirts is made on a special *tubular knitting machine* that makes one long piece of cloth without any seams— just like a long tube. That's why your T-shirt doesn't have any side seams like all of your other shirts have.

The cotton cloth is then dyed with a safe chemical solution in large tanks. It can be bleached so that it becomes a bright white, like most T-shirts, or it can be red, blue, green, or any color you'd like.

This process can take several minutes or a few hours. The cloth and the solution have to be mixed thoroughly so that all of the cloth comes out the same color.

After dyeing, the cloth is pressed and ironed—*calendered*—so that it is flat and has no wrinkles. This is important because someone has to cut out the exact pieces that make up a T-shirt. This job takes skill and care.

The cloth is spread up to ninety-six layers high on long, narrow tables. Then a person called a *cutter*, using a vibrating long knife, follows a pattern to cut the T-shirt pieces through many layers of cloth. Today computers can do all of this, stamping out the pieces of cloth like a huge cookie cutter.

13

Finally all the pieces that go into making a T-shirt—the body, the neck band, the arms—are sewn together by an army of people using small sewing machines. When they are finished, they hem each T-shirt at the bottom, around the neck, and at the end of the sleeves. Hemming prevents all the little cotton fibers from pulling apart.

Each batch of new T-shirts is checked for color and quality. Special machines test the strength of the T-shirts to make sure they are strong and durable. Then they are boxed and sent off to stores all over the country.

But this is where the real fun begins! Not everyone wants a plain white T-shirt—they want theirs to be different from everyone else's.

That's why you can go into a store and have your own message pressed onto the T-shirt.

You can have your name (or your friend's), your favorite team's name, your favorite joke, or a picture of your favorite singer—anything you want! The person in the store just has to heat up an iron, place the decal (the picture or letters) on the T-shirt, press hard, and presto! Here's your very own special T-shirt.

You can do almost anything with a T-shirt. Some people spray them with paint, and others use paintbrushes to create their own works of art. Some people hang things from their T-shirts, and some just leave them plain, the way the shirts came. T-shirts are more adaptable and popular than any other piece of clothing ever invented—everyone seems to wear T-shirts!

What a success story the T-shirt is! Would you believe that the T-shirt began as underwear called *skivvy shirts*—something that was worn under navy uniforms in World War II, just like a vest? At that time, no one would dare wear a T-shirt by itself—that would be like walking around half-dressed.

20

Wearing T-shirts became really popular after two famous actors, Marlon Brando and James Dean, wore them in the movies. Today, fashions and trends are still being set by the movie stars we admire.

So the next time you wake up in the morning and pull your favorite T-shirt over your head, think about all those people it takes to make one T-shirt. But especially think of that beautiful plant with its pink flowers eating up the sunshine and drinking up the rain, just waiting to give us the cotton that clothes us and keeps us warm.

ABOUT
THE
ARTIST

Michael Moran is a
freelance illustrator who
excels at drawing people
with long noses. A
graduate of the School of
Visual Arts in New
York, his work appears
regularly in magazines
and newspapers,
including the *New York
Times* and the *Boston
Globe.*